W9-BQI-028

OCEANS

DONNA LATHAM

Nomad Press
A division of Nomad Communications
10 9 8 7 6 5 4 3 2 1

Printed by Regal Printing Limited in China,
June 2010, Job Number 1005019
ISBN: 978-1-934670-88-0

Questions regarding the ordering of this book should be addressed to
Independent Publishers Group
814 N. Franklin St.
Chicago, IL 60610
www.ipgbook.com

Nomad Press
2456 Christian St.
White River Junction, VT 05001
www.nomadpress.net

Image Credits

corbisimages.com/ Louise Murray, cover; Specialist Stock, 1; Mark A. Johnson, 5; Visuals Unlimited, 14, 15; Jeffrey L. Rotman, 16.

©iStockphoto.com/ Keith Flood, i; Nick M. Do, i; SecondShot, ii; Natallia Bokach, iii; Jan Rysavy, 3; Jussi Santaniemi, 4; Tammy Peluso, 7, 9, 23; Kristen Johansen, 9; Miguel Angelo Silva, 10; John Anderson, 10, 11; Kristian Sekulic, 11; syagci, 11; cbpix, 13; Christopher Meder, 14; Eric Madeja, 17; Joseph Luoman, 18; Malcolm Crooks, 19; Els van der Gun, 19; Tobias Helbig, 20; Deborah Maxemow, 20; Piero Malaer, 21; Jurie Maree, 22; Liz Leyden, 22; David Gomez, 22; Rainer Albiez, 25; Phil Dickson, 26.

Image courtesy of the Monterey Bay Aquarium Research Institute. © 2004 MBARI/ 15.

CONTENTS

What Is a Biome?

Earth is a watery world. Its nickname is the "Blue Planet" because water covers almost three-quarters of its surface.

The ocean is the largest of all the **biomes.** A biome is a large natural area with a distinctive **climate** and **geology.** The desert is a biome. The rainforest is a biome. So is the tundra in the Arctic. Biomes are the earth's communities.

biome: a large natural area with a distinctive climate, geology, and set of water resources. A biome's plants and animals are adapted for life there.

climate: average weather patterns in an area over a period of many years.

geology: the rocks, minerals, and physical structure of an area.

adapt: changes a plant or animal makes to survive in new or different conditions.

ecosystem: a community of living and nonliving things and their environment. Living things are plants, animals, and insects. Nonliving things are soil, rocks, and water.

environment: everything in nature, living and nonliving.

Each biome has its own biodiversity, which is the range of living things **adapted** for life there. It also contains many **ecosystems**. In an ecosystem, living and nonliving things interact with their **environment**.

Teamwork keeps the system balanced and working. Earth's biomes are connected together, creating a vast web of life.

2

Landscape and Climate

Another word for ocean is marine. The marine biome is the salt water surrounding all the continents. It includes the Atlantic, Pacific, Arctic, Indian, and Southern Oceans.

Did You Know?

Scientists don't agree on how many biomes there are. Some divide the earth into 5 biomes. Others argue for 12.

of the Ocean

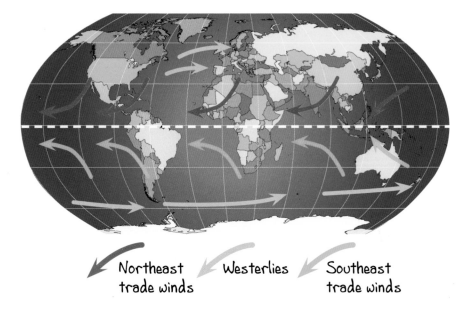

Northeast trade winds   Westerlies   Southeast trade winds

The ocean water is always moving

because of the wind and the way the earth spins as it moves around the sun. Wind is moving air that starts with heat from the sun.

As the sun heats up the land, the air above it heats up and rises. Cooler air over oceans moves in to take the place of the warm air as it rises. This shifting, moving air is the wind.

When wind blows over the ocean, it pushes water on the surface. The water changes shape, forming waves. The stonger the wind, the bigger the waves.

Currents are masses of water that are always on the move!

Ocean currents on the surface are caused by wind and by the earth's spinning. North of the equator in the earth's Northern Hemisphere, circular currents flow in a clockwise direction. South of the equator in the Southern Hemisphere, currents move counterclockwise.

Some scientists compare currents to streams or rivers within the ocean.

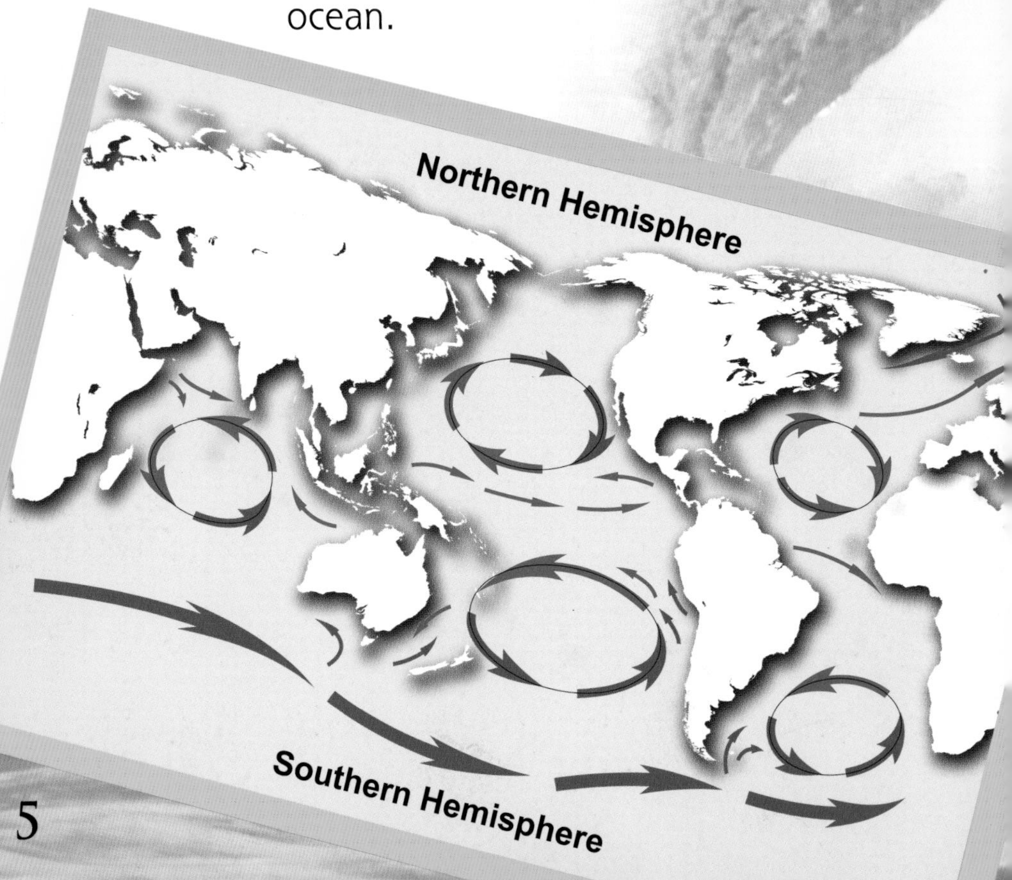

Northern Hemisphere

Southern Hemisphere

The world's tallest known wave clobbered Lituya Bay, Alaska, in 1958. This destructive wave, called a tsunami, towered 1,750 feet (525 meters). That's higher than the Taipei 101 Tower, the world's second-tallest building. Tsunamis are caused by underwater earthquakes.

Although the water of the marine biome is constantly moving and mixing, water temperatures still vary quite a lot depending on location.

Polar waters, in the far north and south near the poles, are as low as a frosty 28 degrees Fahrenheit (-2 degrees Celsius). Tropical waters, close to the equator, are more like 85 degrees Fahrenheit (29 degrees Celsius). The temperature at the bottom of the ocean is much colder than at the surface.

The underwater landscape

is filled with soaring mountains, vast canyons, and many active volcanoes!

The Pacific Ocean's Ring of Fire contains about three-quarters of the earth's volcanoes. The Ring of Fire reaches from the waters off New Zealand and around the Philippines to Alaska and down the coasts of North and South America. Underwater eruptions and earthquakes rock the waves.

Word Exploration

An aquanaut is an underwater explorer. The Latin prefix *aqua* means "water." The Greek suffix *naut* comes from the word nautical. *Naut* means "explorer or voyager." What other words do you know that contain *aqua*? How about *naut*?

Plants Growing in the

Scientists divide the ocean into zones, according to depth and the amount of sunlight each zone receives. When you splash in the waters at the beach, you're in the sunlight zone.

Because plants require sunlight, most ocean plants are found in the sunlight zone. Seagrass, seaweed, and algae are common here.

Ocean Have Adapted

sunlight zone

twilight zone

midnight zone

ocean floor

Colorful coral reefs are amazing examples of **symbiosis**. Coral is a combination of living plants and the skeletons of dead animals.

How do coral reefs form?

These incredible water rainforests start with a **microscopic** animal called a coral polyp. The polyp attaches itself to an underwater rock with its tentacles. Algae living in the coral use it for protection and supply it with food.

Polyps use calcium from sea water to make limestone skeletons over their lower bodies.

When the polyps die, their skeletons become part of the reef. The skeletons are like building blocks that add onto the reef.

It's a slow process—it takes nearly 10,000 years for a coral reef to form!

Words to Know

symbiosis: when two different **species** depend on each other. Each benefits from the other.

species: a type of animal or plant.

microscopic: something so small it can only be seen with a microscope.

Animals Living in the

Nearly all of the ocean's animals also inhabit the sunlight zone.

The shark is a **predator** at the top of the **food chain**. The shark's skin is darker on top of its body than on the bottom. This **camouflage** is an important **adaptation**.

When unsuspecting **prey** darting above the predator peer down, the shark is camouflaged in the dark water below. So the shark can sneak up on its victim and snag the prey. When prey swim under the predator, the shark's lighter-colored bottom camouflages it against bright, sunlight zone waters—and the shark gets the prey again.

What Eats What?

Microscopic plants are at the bottom of the ocean's food chain. Fish eat plants and bigger fish eat smaller fish. Predators like sharks each large fish.

Ocean Have Adapted

predator: an animal that hunts another animal for food.

food chain: a community of animals and plants where each is eaten by another higher up in the chain.

camouflage: colors or patterns that allow a plant or animal to blend in with its environment.

adaptation: physical or behavioral charateristics that help a plant or animal survive.

prey: an animal hunted by a predator for food.

As you descend into the deeper waters of the twilight zone, you'll notice that light is limited. It's a good thing deep-sea creatures are adapted with stellar eyesight! The hatchet fish has bulging, tube-shaped eyes that point up so it can spot food drifting overhead.

The bizarre-looking barrel-eye fish is able to see predators through its transparent head and zip to safety. Then its eyes rotate forward so it can chomp on prey.

How do sea creatures live in total darkness deep in the twilight zone and midnight zone of the ocean? With extreme adaptations! Bioluminescence is an adaptation that allows squid, flashlight fish, and anglerfish to glow in the dark using special chemicals present in their bodies.

The vampire squid has webbing that flutters out from behind it like Dracula's cape. Photophores cover its

body. These are organs that produce light. The vampire squid can turn on its lights to attract mates and prey, as well as startle and temporarily blind predators.

16

Environmental Threats

Climate change and global warming threaten the earth's oceans as much as the land biomes. Rising water temperatures affect ecosystems. One example is the danger faced by coral reefs.

Warmer waters stress sensitive coral. When stressed, coral tosses out algae, which provides coral's dazzling colors as well as food for its survival. The coral starves to death. Drained of vibrant color, it looks bleached.

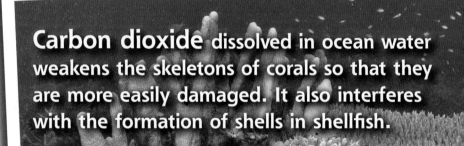

Carbon dioxide dissolved in ocean water weakens the skeletons of corals so that they are more easily damaged. It also interferes with the formation of shells in shellfish.

Oil Spills cause great damage to ocean ecosystems. Every oil spill poisons sea life and ruins coastlines.

Trash is another huge threat to our oceans. An immense island of floating garbage—double the size of Texas—drifts aimlessly in the Pacific Ocean between California and Hawaii. This "trash stew" of tattered plastic bags, bobbing pellets, smashed toys, and bits of plastic bottles threatens animal life.

Dolphins, albatrosses, and other seabirds get tangled in bags or mistakenly gobble down plastic pellets. Toxins in the plastics poison animal life. The trash causes severe injuries and even death through choking or clogged intestines.

In the vast, interconnected web of life, people are impacted by trash and pollutants in the oceans, too. Fish eat the plant life that floats in the toxic waters. Then we eat the fish that have consumed the toxins.

Biodiversity at Risk

Many plants and animals are endangered. And when an animal or plant species becomes extinct, that means it's gone forever. There are many causes of **extinction**. Natural occurrences, such as volcanic eruptions, have caused extinctions in the past.

Today, marine animals may become extinct when they are overhunted or when their **habitat** is destroyed or damaged. Overhunting whales in the 1800s for whale oil put many species of whale at risk.

Even though whales have been protected for years, they still get hit by ships and tangled up in fishing nets. Drilling for oil and gas in their feeding grounds disrupts the whale's life cycle.

then: Sea otters once called the entire west coast of North America home.

now: The last sea otter in Oregon was killed more than 100 years ago. Because they were overhunted for their fur in the past, sea otters are endangered today.

Path to Extinction

Rare: Only a small number of the species is alive. Scientists are concerned about the future of the species.

Threatened: The species lives, but its numbers will likely continue to decline. It will probably become endangered.

Endangered: The species is in danger of extinction in the very near future.

Extinct in the Wild: Some members of the species live, but only in protected captivity and not out in the wild.

Extinct: The species has completely died out. It has disappeared from the planet.

The Future of the Ocean

Loss of habitat, the spread of disease, pollution, and overfishing are some of the threats facing endangered species today.

When natural or manmade disasters like volcanic eruptions or oil spills take place in one biome, they often have an effect on other biomes as well. People are increasingly aware of the delicate balance of life on Earth. Many are devoted to conserving our natural resources and preserving our biomes.

Conservation Challenge

Think about what You can do to help the ocean environment. Make a poster with some ideas.

- Reduce, reuse, recyle. Trash contaminates our oceans and precious beaches. What can you do about it? Cut down on your use of plastic products, and always recycle as much plastic as possible. Plastic is forever.

- Try to use less energy. The less you drive or the less electricity you use, the better. We all use energy made from oil.

- Fertilize with organic products that won't harm the environment. The water that runs off your yard ends up in rivers and streams that empty into the ocean.

- Buy only sustainably harvested seafood. That means choosing fish that is not in danger of being overfished.

Did You Know?

Scientists studying a dead bird discovered a bit of plastic in its stomach. The plastic contained a serial number. That number came from a World War II plane that was gunned down over the Pacific Ocean in 1944. Plastic really does last a long time.

Glossary

adapt: changes a plant or animal makes to survive in new or different conditions.

adaptation: physical or behavioral characteristics that help a plant or animal survive.

biodiversity: the range of living things in an ecosystem.

biome: a large natural area with a distinctive climate, geology, and water resources. A biome's plants and animals are adapted for life there.

camouflage: colors or patterns that allow a plant or animal to blend in with its environment.

carbon dioxide: a gas that contributes to global warming.

climate: average weather patterns in an area over a period of many years.

climate change: a change in the world's weather and climate.

current: constantly moving mass of water.

ecosystem: a community of living and nonliving things and their environment. Living things are plants, animals, and insects. Nonliving things are soil, rocks, and water.

environment: everything in nature, living and nonliving.

extinction: the death of an entire species so that it no longer exists.

food chain: a community of animals and plants where each is eaten by another higher up in the chain.

geology: the rocks, minerals, and physical structure of an area.

global warming: the rise in the world's temperature that leads to climate change.

habitat: a plant or animal's home.

microscopic: something so small it can only be seen with a microscope.

midnight zone: the ocean zone that gets no light.

predator: an animal that hunts another animal for food.

prey: an animal hunted by a predator for food.

species: a type of animal or plant.

sunlight zone: the ocean zone that sunlight penetrates, where plants can grow.

symbiosis: when two different species depend on each other. Each benefits from the other.

tsunami: an abnormally large, destructive wave caused by an underwater earthquake.

twilight zone: the ocean zone reached by very little or no sunlight.

Further Investigations

Cherry, Lynn. *How We Know What We Know About Our Changing Climate: Scientists and Kids Explore Global Warming*. Dawn Publications, 2008.

Latham, Donna. *Amazing Biome Projects You Can Build Yourself*. Nomad Press, 2009.

Reilly, Kathleen M. *Planet Earth: 25 Environmental Projects You Can Build Yourself*. Nomad Press, 2008.

Rothschild, David. *Earth Matters: An Encyclopedia of Ecology*. DK Publishing, 2008.

Smithsonian Institution National Museum of Natural History
www.mnh.si.edu
Washington, D.C.

US National Parks www.us-parks.com

Enchanted Learning, Biomes
www.enchantedlearning.com/biomes

Energy Efficiency and Renewable Energy
www.eere.energy.gov/kids

Geography for Kids www.kidsgeo.com

Inch in a Pinch: Saving the Earth
www.inchinapinch.com

Kids Do Ecology
www.kids.nceas.ucsb.edu

Library ThinkQuest
www.thinkquest.org

National Geographic Kids
www.kids.nationalgeographic.com

NOAA for Kids
www.oceanservice.noaa.gov/kids

Oceans for Youth
www.oceansforyouth.org

The Nature Conservancy
www.nature.org

World Wildlife Federation
www.panda.org

Index